Fraud Inspectors

Fraud Inspectors

Table Of Contents

Foreword

Con artists who push scams have a crucial factor working for them besides the sorry state of our economic system, and that's the lack of a uniform, comprehensive, national clamp down by law enforcement officials.

It's exceedingly hard to track, shut down, and bring these rogue companies to justice, as many will confirm today. And because most consumers wind up getting taken for a relatively little sum of money, attorneys are seldom willing or able to get involved, nor do local law enforcement representatives.

According to the Better Business Council, only twenty-three % of the bureaus responding to a survey reported any law enforcement actions taken against scams in their area, in spite of the fact that ninety-three % of the bureaus around the country have got complaints about scams.

Here we will show you what these are and how to avoid them.

Scam Busters

How To Avoid The Most Popular Scams Of Today!

Chapter 1:

Synopsis

There are popular scams anybody ought to avoid when trying to work from home. There are constantly individuals attempting to beat any system by doing things lawlessly. Never before has this been more true than with the net and Unemployment.

Nowadays, millions of Americans battle with unemployment. As long as there's a high level of unemployment, there will be elevated levels of predators looking to target individuals at their most vulnerable moment.

Small Business Predators

A few consumers have lost 1000s of dollars on these scams, but the ordinary victim gets taken for about forty bucks. Now, that might not seem like a lot of cash, but to the distressed family, it is a lot. And, naturally, it's also heartbreak and an embarrassment too.

When you total it up, from the point of view of the work-at-home swindle artists, it's a multimillion-dollar rip-off of people around the globe. These are not individuals who want something for nothing, the people who are replying to these ads. They're decent individuals who wish to work and whose conditions make them susceptible to work-at-home scams.

There is a growing issue of work-at-home scams.

These scams capitalize on the eagerness of individuals to earn cash by doing work at home. People drew in to these offers are, more often than not, willing to do truthful work for truthful pay. They simply find it hard, occasionally impossible, to hold a job outside their home because of family responsibilities, health circumstances, or lack of training.

Too frequently work-at-home scams are brushed aside as petty nuisances. Bureaus report that the sum of money lost by a work-at-home victim ranges anyplace from $5 to 100s of dollars, with the average, is as stated, hovering around $40.

That doesn't sound like a substantial sum of money; however it may represent a week's worth of groceries to a victim. And it is not strange for an individual to fall victim to 2 or 3 or 4 such scams before they finally recognize that they're not going to get real employment from such offers.

It is not strange for even the most respectable papers and magazines to run ads for work-at-home schemes. Publishers have the might to block such ads, but only a few do. A lot of BBB's offer help to local publications to check into the legitimacy of such offers prior to publication.

The most beneficial piece of advice I may offer to those interested in going after work-at-home opportunities is to cautiously evaluate any such marketing and to check it out with the local Better Business Bureau to determine the reputation of the company. Consumers shouldn't presume that the offer doesn't warrant checking into because it involves only a small fee. That's the attitude that allows work-at-home scam artists to prosper.

Here are the top 10 popular scams to keep away from when attempting to work from home.

- The Rebate Processing Scam
- Online Search Scam
- Envelope Stuffing Scam
- Government Grant Scam
- Work from Home Assembling Crafts Scam
- Medical Billing Scam
- Pre Screened List of Jobs Scam
- Mystery Shopper Scam
- Money Laundering Scam

- Promise of Employment with the Federal Government Scam

It's unfortunate that we now have individuals that have the heart to capitalize on people who would like to earn a great income from the web. But the existence of work from home scams is certainly an indicator that a lot of people are already being duped by these scammers.

If you're someone that's seeking a work at home prospect, you probably would like to know if there's a way to spot these work from home scams and prevent being scammed. The reality is that you are able to find the answer.

You simply need to be sensitive to particular clues that may tell you just how the site you're considering is a work at home scam.

__Below are a few of the long-familiar qualities of work from home scam sites:__

Shabby web site individuals state that you merely can't judge a book by its cover but it's likewise correct that the clothes make the man and in that case, a site design might provide you a lot of hints about a work from home opportunity. Once a site seems like it absolutely was hastily produced by some talentless fool then it's obviously a work from home scam.

Incorrect grammar and a few misspelled words are likewise telltale signals that the web site you're looking at is not at all real. Solely align yourself with companies that have a professional looking site. When they're not professional enough to make a respectable site then they're likely work from home scams.

If a site asks cash from you upfront without revealing first the benefits of signing up with them chances are they're commonly a work from home scam masked as a reputable web site. If they trust in their product or service so much then they'll be prepared to let you give it a shot first.

<u>Spam</u>

No honorable business would ever employ spamming as a strategy for advertising. If a company utilizes spam, it's truly a work from home scam.

Chapter 2:

Debt Relief Scams

Synopsis

The heist is the upfront fee you pay to have the company talk terms with lenders — which commonly does not occur; so not only are you out the fee, but your debts have amassed more interest and penalties.

Hang Onto Your Cash

The long, thick recession and its aftermath have produced an environment in which debt reduction scams and debt relief scams prosper. With millions in money trouble, charge card debt is a bigger issue than ever.

Vulturous debt relief companies promising serenity are seeking out individuals drowning in debt. However with financial discipline and effort individuals may stay away from even the alleged legitimate debt reduction services.

Debt reducing booby traps

Paying back existing debts with more debt is a common maneuver of companies hawking debt reducing services. Additional debt reduction services will offer to talk terms with your creditors to arrange a pay back for under what you owe.

In a lot of cases simply taking your upfront fee is all that counts, not really reducing your debt. And one thing they won't explain to you is that paying less than you owe presents on your credit report as failure to pay off your debt in full, which plays havoc on your credit score.

Debt easing in disguise

That financial marauders sell themselves as legitimate companies with the power to help consumers overpowered by charge card debt is no secret. The Los Angeles Times describes that investigators for the Government Accountability Office acted as distressed consumers looking for help from debt management companies. Devising wild exaggerations of their success rates, a few companies promised savings of as much as 1/2.

Debt reducing fake promises

After paying up big up-front fees to debt management companies, frequently running up to a thousand dollars, many consumers wind up deeper in debt than they were previously. One woman in North Carolina fell for the sales pitch from a debt relief company that she would maintain enough with lower interest rates to settle charge cards, a mortgage and an auto loan 5 times faster.

After paying $ 599 up front, she was promised that interest rate savings would make up for the fee inside the first thirty days on her way to a complete savings of $ 2,500. The FTC sued the firm after they declined to refund the $ 599 fee after neglecting to deliver on those promises.

A basic debt relief ruse

Laying claim as "government approval" is a basic angle engaged by debt relief scam artists nowadays. The Los Angeles Times reported that statements made by debt management companies to GAO researchers, as well as their advertisements, show the firms attempt leading people to believe they're administrators of a government plan related to the bank bailout.

One business that surfaces at the top of search engine rankings for debt relief names itself the Federal Debt Relief Program. A more less-than-honest scam is the "U.S. National Debt Relief Plan.

Debt relief – DIY

There are 100s of debt reduction and debt relief companies invading the net, but there's no government-backed charge card debt relief plan. Debt relief in these disruptive times has become a big industry co-opted by shysters capitalizing on desperate people.

Getting on a spending budget that lets you pay your bills promptly and pay down your debt is nonetheless the most beneficial route to debt relief. Negotiating greater terms or lower payments and refinancing car or house loans are actions you're able to take yourself.

Debt management advice—free of charge

For assistance with debt troubles, the National Foundation for Credit Counseling is a great place to begin. Anyone who requires free and confidential advice about debt relief may get it from this non-profit-making community group.

The NFCC provides consulting in person or by telephone. To find a counselor in your community go to nfcc.org.

Chapter 3:

Synopsis

Like debt relief scams, alleged foreclosure companies offer to get your mortgage altered — after you send them a humongous fee. No adjustments happen; homeowners fall farther behind and go thicker in debt.

According to ConsumerAffairs.com, the Indiana Attorney General alone filed thirty-four lawsuits against these companies. Like firms pledge to modify car loans with the same non-result.

Real Property

Refinancing is a way by which you are able to substitute an elevated rate loan with a lower rate commercial mortgage so that you're comfortable paying back the debt on your house. But while you go for a mortgage refinance, be mindful of the fact that you don't easily fall prey to a refinancing scam and wind up losing 1000s of dollars. As then you might require serious debt help.

Here are three refinancing scams you ought to be aware of if you'd like to prevent being a fraud victim:

Greater balances or payments:

Marauding lenders would attempt to push you into greater balances or payments if you refinance your mortgage. Such lenders might even allow you to borrow more than what you ought to be provided. This is frequently done by inflating the assessment on your home. The chief aim of such scammers is to take out more interest from you. And then if you default, the lender will take your home.

The better way to avoid this is to collect a few details of the lender's services and the refinance loan plan that's being offered to you and ask as many questions as conceivable.

Not supplying suitable disclosures:

There are lenders who don't disclose every detail about the loan plan that he might provide you. It's better to stand back from lenders who delays or refuses to supply information. Such lenders might even ask you for buried charges and additional fees which you shouldn't be paying in reality.

Asking you to make payment on blank forms:

Frequently lenders ask you to sign on forms thereby stating that they'll fill the blank spaces later on. It's better to keep away from signing on such forms which have blank spaces. And, do read through the whole form before signing.

If you'd like to make your refinance deal a winner, look out for the refinancing scams and prevent making errors while you're seeking the right loan that will help suit your needs.

Lately, the incidence of mortgage scams has expanded manifold. Not everybody may qualify to get a mortgage loan. Frequently it has been observed that loan officers step-up the income of the "subprime" purchasers so that they may qualify to receive a loan.

The manipulation is accepted by the purchasers too as they've the greed of their property being valued at a greater price than what it is in reality. The mortgage lenders on the other hand get a greater commission. It likewise leads to rampant adjustable rate mortgage loan scams.

Recently, there has been a growth in the number of foreclosures. A lot of unsuspecting investors suffered big losses owing to manipulation by real property operators at assorted levels.

Reports propose that a leading seller of CMO or collateral mortgage responsibilities sold approximately USD$100 billion worth of CMOs to investors.

Passed on below are a few of the widely practiced mortgage scams which finally result in adjustable rate mortgage loan scams also.

Fraud to qualify-

The debtor supplies fake data about himself. It might include his income, employment history, how he's sourcing his down payment and his purpose of occupancy of the property.

Silent second-

Silent second is a sort of fraud when the seller lends out some cash to the purchaser so that the intending purchaser may make the down payment. An unrecorded or a "silent" second mortgage supplies the essential fund for the down payment.

The lender is of the belief that the cash belongs to the purchaser. This scenario commonly misrepresents the actual financial condition of the intending purchaser.

Fraud for profit- It includes scams in which industry insiders like lenders, closing lawyers, real estate brokers and appraisers are equally involved.

There are versions of this sort of mortgage fraud but a few of the basic forms are presented below-

Straw purchasers-

Straw purchasers are referred to as people who are utilized to hide the identity of the real borrower. Straw purchasers commonly have a great credit history. They're made to believe that they're actually investing in real estate property that will be rented out.

They're commonly given the impression that the rent will be utilized to make mortgage payments. They're likewise a party in the fraud as they make profit from net income.

Flipping –

In home flipping, houses are bought which undergo renovation or betterment and they're resold again. This yields fast profits and the seller conceals the true value of the property and gets the property incorrectly appraised.

Foreclosure scams- A person who's in the initial stages of foreclosure is approached by a scammer shamming to help the person so that the home may be saved from foreclosure. The scammer commonly takes an upfront fee and vanishes. There's another version of this scam.

A person whose home is in the early stages of foreclosure is approached by a scammer who advises techniques to refinance the mortgage. The scammer makes the person sign papers. The person discovers that he's actually sold the home to the scammer.

Appraisal sham-

The property value is appraised to a great extent. An appraiser commonly does this. The seller gets his dues and makes payment to the appraiser affected. But, the debtor is not able to dish out this elevated amount and the home goes into foreclosure.

Knowing how to recognize all of these can help you to avoid them.

Chapter 4:

You Won Scams

Synopsis

The target, frequently an elderly individual, gets a telephone call or letter announcing that he's won 1000000s from a foreign lottery, Publishers Clearinghouse or Reader's Digest. To acquire the cash, all the same, he has to wire hundreds or even thousands of bucks to cover a phony fee or taxes. No prize ever happens.

Where Is The Prize

Scam operators — frequently based in the Netherlands, Canada and Federal Republic of Nigeria— are utilizing the phone, net and direct mail to tempt U.S. (and other global) consumers to purchase chances in high-stakes foreign lotteries from as far-off as Australia and Europe.

<u>There are a lot of different sorts of lottery scams:</u>

- A lottery notifies you (e-mail, mail or telephone) that you won*, or
- You travel to a lottery site, or by telephone or mail to "play" / purchase a ticket, or
- You purchase a "program" of "secrets" on how to win drawings.
- Green card (immigration VISA) lottery
- Sweepstakes scams (Sweepstakes are not really a lottery, but are frequently confused with them)

Remember, no legitimate lottery will ever send word to you that you won. They don't work that way!

Contrary to a sweepstakes, a lottery is a promotional device by which particulars of value (prizes) are awarded to members of the public by luck, but which requires some form of payment to participate. Put differently, if you didn't purchase a ticket, you could NOT have WON a lottery - regardless what anybody tells you!

Lotteries in the U.S., Canada, Australia and UK, and most developed countries, are illegal, except if carried on by states and particular exempt licensed charitable organizations. If you trust you've received a solicitation in the guise of a sweepstake which is an illegal lottery, you ought to contact your post office or state Attorney General's consumer protection office

Victims commonly are notified they've won a lottery, yet have to pay transference fees, taxes or supply proof of their identity and/or details of their bank accounts or charge card in order to get the "winnings".

The names of these organizations shift all the time (they simply make up a fresh name when one is exposed as a fraud), while many of the notifications utilize like wording.

Here are chief points for warding off scam lotteries:

- You can't win a legitimate lottery if you haven't entered it.
- In almost all cases you have to buy a ticket to enter a legitimate drawing.
- You never have to pay to garner winnings from a licit lottery. You pay taxes following getting winning there are no additional fees.
- If you have a winning lottery ticket, you notify the lottery (they don't notify you; not by e-mail, not by telephone, not by mail).
- It's illegal under U.S. federal law to play whatever foreign lottery from the U.S.. A lot of additional countries have similar laws. For instance, you must be a Spanish resident to play the El Gordo lottery.
- As scammers merely invent fresh names for their fake e-mail scam (the e-mail is the scam, not any individuals or companies named in the e-mail)s, it is more exact to say that if you don't

see the lottery on the list of legitimate lotteries, it's probably a scam.

- If it isn't conducted by a government or government-authorized charitable organization, it can't be a licit lottery

But how did they acquire my name, if not through a lottery I entered?

Names and addresses of likely victims are harvested by malware, viruses and additional tools and gotten rough assorted trade journals, business directories, magazine and newspaper ads chambers of commerce, and anyplace your name appears on the net (such as in chat rooms, forums, and so forth.). They may simply wont a telephone directory for your country, either online or the paper variety.

But it may be a legal lottery, correct? Legitimate lotteries don't utilize e-mail to notify their winners. In almost all cases, it's up to the holder of the ticket to get hold of the lottery. And even if these were legitimate, these drawing solicitations violate U.S. law, which forbids the cross-border sale or purchase of lottery tickets by telephone or mail. And in the U.S., if it isn't run by a state government or authorized charitable organization, it can't be a lawful lottery!

Net lotteries are illegal in a lot of other countries, too: All lotteries, including foreign lotteries functioning in Great Britain, are unlawful in the UK (except those provided for by the 1976 Lotteries and Amusements Act; meaning government run lotteries). A few of these lottery schemes state that the Gaming Board for UK has approved them, but this isn't true. The Gaming Board has a list of these companies and lotteries on its site, and warns individuals not to take part in them.

What are lottery and prize scams?

These are notifications that advise individuals that they've won a prize (frequently for a competition they didn't even enter).

How to spot a prize or lottery scam

Check the name of the lottery or sweepstakes versus a list of scammer names.

Bear the accompanying warning signs in mind:

If the prize or lottery notice bears any of the following components, we powerfully propose you don't respond to it:

- The info advises that you've won a prize - however you didn't enter any contest run by the prize promoters.
- The mail might be personally addressed to you but it has been placed utilizing bulk mail - 1000s of other people around the world might have received the exact same notification.
- You're frequently asked for cash up front to release your 'win'.
- The prize promoters require a fee (for administration or "processing") to be paid beforehand.
- You're asked for your bank account, charge card details or additional confidential info
- The caller is more frantic than you or the stranger who telephones wishes to be your best friend

- You're told you must reply at once or the cash will be given to somebody else.
- Additional schemes pretend to be legitimate lotteries, or provide you the chance to purchase shares in a fund that purports to buy tickets in legitimate overseas lotteries.
- The scheme provides bait prizes that, if they're real, are frequently substandard, over-priced, or falsely presented. Or, as part of the prize you are able to buy "exclusive items" which may likewise be over-priced or substandard.
- To get your prize may require travel overseas at your own cost to get it.

What will the scammer say when you call their telephone number.
Ok, we've just said that there's NO SUCH THING as a lawful lottery that "picked out your e-mail from a database" or a "PC ballot system"; which means these individuals are criminals working a con. And you still wish to contact them? So, we know you likely also believe in UFO's, and the tooth fairy.

The Bottom Line: What you have to understand

If you get a "prize notification" from a lottery:

- Don't respond to the e-mails
- Don't EVER pay any cash beforehand to collect a prize
- Don't divulge your full identity
- Don't divulge any financial or personal info, like your bank account number or charge card details.

Chapter 5:

Synopsis

You might already know about phishing (which sends you an e-mail leading to a replica of a bank site, where you supply your SSN and account numbers), but now there's vishing (same deal merely with net based phones) and smishing (utilization of texting and cell calls to once again lead you to a phony web site where you tell all).

The messages indicate that something is haywire with your bank account, and you have to immediately contact by pressing a number or clicking a url. Once you get there, a machine-driven system elicits the info, and so long identity.

Be Careful About Info

Protection scam artists are making a killing, cashing in on our fears about PC security.

They're pumping out scare ware platforms in the thousands, lighting up bogus warnings claiming our PCs have been tainted with viruses and then demanding a charge to remove them.

Others send protection spaham (misspelled intentionally) messages, deceitfully claiming they may better our online security, provide credit protection and decrease the risk of identity theft.

Let's begin with scare ware -- virus protection scams that typically flash warnings on our PC screens either claiming the machines bear infections or providing a "free" scan to see if you're infected (which, naturally, they'll state you are).

These might be of the pop-up window assortment, appearing during net browsing, or, more lately, they might mimic the so-called Blue Screen of Death on PCs (not Macs) which tells you your PC has crashed.

You're then invited to purchase a license for a downloadable platform with a genuine-sounding name, occasionally similar to established, bona fide software.

The price is commonly around $40, but the platform doesn't work. Worse still, it might even download additional malicious software onto your PC -- stuff that might steal personal info from your hard drive.

It might even install ransom ware -- platforms that make some of your data inaccessible till you pay a ransom fee.

There are more than 9,000 assortments of these scare ware platforms, promoted by networks of hackers and other crooks that get a fee every time they hook a dupe.

Lately, we've seen scare ware links embedded in remarks about videos on YouTube and in "tweets" on Twitter.

Or you might get a message offering to update a legitimate piece of software on your PC (a Flash player for instance), when it's truly a scare ware download.

In additional cases, protection scams lurk on pirated web pages (500,000 of them in one recent count), search results on Google, ads and additional net services.

Whatever the road, they all end in that infection warning and download invitation and, in a lot of cases, even if you suspect a scam, you can't close the warning window without launching a different one. As a matter of fact, you might not even be able to close your browser. As one authority put it: It's like a walk in quicksand.

So how may you protect yourself from scare ware? Here are a few crucial tips:

- Most importantly, install legitimate Internet security software from the likes of Symantec, McAfee, Trend, AVG, or Kaspersky. Hunt it out yourself -- don't reply to protection spaham. These platforms will alert you to scare ware.

- Scanning your entire system ought to likewise remove any protection scam platforms that have already found their way onto your machine.

- 2nd, never click on a pop-up that lays claim your PC is infected or offers a free of charge scan. They're virtually all protection scams. Period. Don't even click on the "no thanks" or "X" close box in such cases -- after all, this is a scam, a click is a click, and you may wind up downloading malware.

- Rather, close your browser. If you can't "X" out of it, right click (on a PC) on the program icon in the taskbar and select "Close."

- If that does not work, hold down the Control-Alt-Delete keys to boot Windows Task Manager and then, under the Applications tab, choose the browser and select "End task."

And a few other scare ware points to watch for:

In one version, the pop-up message claims you've an error in your system registry or additional part of your installation (or it offers to scan for these errors) and, once again, offers to put it right for a charge. Don't fall for it.

There's a branch of scare ware called "prank software," or "prank ware," which is truly just a hoax intended to scare you. A spooky graphic might open on your screen or you might receive a frightening dialog box that states something like "Delete all files on your disk drive?" with only an "OK" button.

This is somebody's idea of a practical joke. Ignore it and close your browser as explained above. And then run your anti-virus scan.

Now let's take a look at ID theft protection scams.

These take a number of sorts, the 3 most common of which are:

You receive a protection spam which seems to come from a legitimate source. A famous late illustration was utilization of the "Verified by Visa" tag in a message that invited users to register for this scheme (which does really exist) by clicking on a link that took them to a spoof page where they were supposed to list all their charge card details!

Genuine ID protection corporations don't spaham, so never reply to such messages. Rather, if you're concerned, do your own search; seek established reputable companies.

You receive an e-mail or telesales call telling you your name has arrived on a list of potential ID theft targets, or even that your net identity has been compromised.

Frequently, the caller or e-mail writer will claim to have a security-related title, like "inspector" and will offer you protection for a charge -- commonly $300

Once again, this is bogus. Everybody is a potential ID theft target.

If your info was on a stolen laptop computer or other compromised device, you'll be contacted through snail mail, not by e-mail or phone -- and you'll frequently be presented some free service protection (instead of be asked to buy protection).

Somebody offers to remove your personal details from the net, thereby cutting back the risk of identity theft.

This is a "no-can-do" protection scam. You can't wipe out all of your personal details from the countless sources, many of them public records, available on the net. (It's possible to remove your details from case-by-case sources though.) Don't believe anybody who states otherwise.

We can't emphasize enough how crucial it is to take steps to protect your identity online and there are lots of valuable things you truly can do in that direction, including working with true identity theft protection services.

Protection scam tricks aren't going to go away anytime soon, so make certain you take the steps defined above to take care of yourself.

Wrapping Up

And one final place to watch out for scams...

Even as young men hop from club to club in pursuit of young ladies to ogle, so too have scammers and hackers accompanied their prey from MySpace to Facebook. As a result, the social network once deemed the "safe" choice is now plagued by legions of 419 scammers, phishers, and peddlers of spyware.

Luckily, there are a few easy rules Facebookers may follow to remain safe: Never Click suspicious links from friends; utilize a service like LongURL before following any abbreviated links; and assume that anybody begging for cash is up to no good. And if you do happen to fall victim to a scam, promptly alert your acquaintances (to prevent spreading the damage), and then alert Facebook administrators and, if it's severe, law enforcement too.

Follow the tips in this book and simply use common sense and you will be able to be safer from people who are out to scam you.

www.ingramcontent.com/pod-product-compliance
Lightning Source LLC
LaVergne TN
LVHW041257200726
843507LV00013B/3022